THE JOKE BOX

A Hilarious Collection of Laughter

Volume IV

This book belongs to:

_____

_____

ABOUT KODE SCRIPT

Welcome to Kode Script, a dynamic publishing company dedicated to crafting digital stories with precision.

At Kode Script, we believe in the transformative power of creativity and education. Specializing in a diverse range of publications, from enchanting coloring books that spark imagination to mind-teasing riddles and puzzles for all ages, we cater to children, adults, and senior individuals alike.

Our mission is to seamlessly blend entertainment with learning, providing enriching experiences through meticulously designed content. With a commitment to quality and innovation, Kode Script invites you to embark on a journey where every page tells a story and every puzzle unveils a new adventure.

If you like our books, please provide your positive reviews on Amazon or any other marketplace. your support will motivate us to do better.

 email : info@kodescript.com   www.kodescript.com

What do you call a line of men waiting for a haircut?

A barberqueue.

What do lawyers wear to court?

Lawsuits!

Why was the turkey in the pop group?

Because he was the only one with drumsticks!

What did the policeman say to his belly button?

You're under a vest!

What do you call a fake noodle?

An impasta.

Why was the baby strawberry crying?

Because his mom and dad were in a jam.

What do you call a boomerang that does not come back?

A stick.

Why wouldn't the shrimp share his treasure?

Because he was a little shellfish.

What did one toilet say to the other toilet?

You look flushed.

Why was the snowman looking through the carrots?

He was picking his nose.

Why is there a gate around cemeteries?

Because people are dying to get in!

Why shouldn't you write with a broken pencil?

Because it's pointless.

What kind of hair does a beach have?

Wavy.

What lights up a soccer stadium?

A soccer match.

What do you call four bullfighters standing in quicksand?

Quattro Sinko.

What does the sun drink out of?

Sunglasses.

Why did the barber win the race?

Because he took a short cut.

Why did the man put his money in the freezer?

He wanted cold hard cash!

What do you call a fish without an eye?

Fsh.

What lies at the bottom of the ocean and twitches?

A nervous wreck.

How do you make a tissue dance?

Put a little boogey in it!

What kind of photos do teeth take?

Toothpics!

What do call cheese that isn't yours?

Nacho Cheese.

How do you make a venetian blind.

Poke him in the eyes.

I was going to tell a joke about fishing... But I forgot the line.

Why couldn't the pony sing himself a lullaby?

He was a little hoarse.

What do you call bears with no ears?

B.

Jokes about air conditioners?

Not a fan.

What do you call a sleeping bull?

A bulldozer!

What do you call a dog that does magic tricks?

A labracadabrador.

What do you call a belt with a watch on it?

A waist of time.

What did the judge say when the skunk walked in the court room?

Odor in the court.

What's it called when a chameleon can't change its colors anymore?

A reptile dysfunction.

Where do pencils go for vacation?

Pencil-vania.

What bow can't be tied?

A rainbow!

Why did the cross-eyed teacher get fired?

She couldn't control her pupils.

How do hens cheer for their team?

They egg them on!

Where do snowmen keep their money?

In snow banks!

What is the difference between girl spaghetti and man spaghetti?

Meatballs.

What is the best day to go to the beach?

Sunday, of course!

What season is it when you are on a trampoline?

Spring time.

Why did the man with one hand cross the road?

To get to the second hand shop.

Where do the poor meatballs live?

The sphaghetto!

Where did the computer go to dance?

To a disc-o.

Why did the birdie go to the hospital?

To get a tweetment.

What did the sweet potato wear to bed?

His pa-yam-as.

What is red and smells like blue paint?

Red Paint.

Why do fish live in salt water?

Because pepper makes them sneeze!

As a wizard, I like turning things into glass. I just wanted to make that clear.

Why is England the wettest country?
Because the queen has reigned there for years!

What has one head, one foot and four legs?
A Bed.

What do you call a blind dinosaur?
Do-you-think-he-saurus.

How do you shoot a killer bee?

With a bee-bee gun.

Why did Roger go out with a prune?

Because he couldn't find a date!

Did you hear the joke about the
broken submarine?

It didn't go down well.

Why did the banana go to the Doctor?

Because it was not peeling well.

Why did the computer go to the doctor?

Because it had a virus!

How do you know when the moon has enough to eat?

When it's full.

Who earns a living driving their customers away?

A taxi driver.

What happened to the dog that swallowed a firefly?

It barked with de-light!

What do you call a pig that knows karate?

Pork Chop.

What kind of dogs like car racing?

Lap dogs.

Why did the girl smear peanut butter on the road?

To go with the traffic jam!

What do you give a cannibal that shows up late to dinner?

A cold shoulder.

What did the little mountain say to the big mountain?

Hi Cliff!

What did Winnie The Pooh say to his agent?

Show me the honey!

What do you call a police officer in bed?

An undercover cop!

Why was there thunder and lightning in the lab?

The scientists were brainstorming!

What goes through towns, up & over hills, but doesn't move?

The road!

What does a Mexican cow call his friends?

MOO-chacho.

What did one elevator say to the other elevator?

I think I'm coming down with something!

Where do bees go to the bathroom?

At the BP station!

Why did the pizza maker run from the mafia?

He owed them a lot of dough!

Why couldn't the pirate play cards?

Because he was sitting on the deck!

What do you call a baby monkey?

A Chimp off the old block.

Why did the skeleton sleep in the snow last night?

He was a numbskull.

What do you get when you cross fish and an elephant?

Swimming trunks.

Why did the traffic light turn red?

You would too if you had to change in the middle of the street!

What do you call clumsy grapes?

Unconcordinated.

What kind of animal do you not want to play games with?

A cheetah.

What word is always spelled wrong in the Dictionary?

Wrong.

What streets do ghosts live on?

Dead Ends!

What do you call the security guards who work at the Samsung store?

Guardians of the Galaxy.

What do you get when you cross a snowman with a vampire?

Frostbite.

Why does the vampire always get picked last?

Because he sucks.

Why did the chicken get a penalty?

For fowl play!

Why couldn't the bicycle stand up by itself?

It was two-tired!

Why was the sand wet?

The sea weed.

What kind of bird sticks to sweaters?

a Vel-Crow.

What did the blanket say to the bed?

Don't worry, I've got you covered!

What is a cheerleader's favorite drink?

Rootbeer.

When does Friday come before Thursday?

In the dictionary.

What washes up on very small beaches?

Microwaves.

How many tickles does it take to make an Octopus laugh?

Ten-tickles.

What's easy to get into but hard to get out of?

Trouble.

What pet makes the loudest noise?

A trum-pet!

What kind of button won't unbutton?

A bellybutton!

Where do boats go when they get sick?

The dock.

What do you call two fat people having a chat?

A heavy discussion.

What do you call a funny mountain?

Hill-arious!

Which month do soldiers hate most?

The month of March!

What did the digital clock say to the grandfather clock?

Look grandpa, no hands!

What did the triangle say to the circle?

You're pointless!

What kind of crackers do firefighters like in their soup?

Firecrackers!

What did the judge say to the dentist?

Do you swear to pull the tooth, the whole tooth and nothing but the tooth.

What is an astronaut's favorite place on a computer?

The Space bar!

Which is the longest word in the dictionary?

"Smiles", because there is a mile between each 's'.

Why did the scarecrow win an award?

Because he was out-standing in his field.

What starts with a P, ends with an E,
and has a million letters in it?

Post Office!

What runs but doesn't get anywhere?

A refrigerator.

Why did the dinosaur cross the road?

**Because the chicken joke wasn't
invented yet.**

What kind of dog keeps the best time?

A watch dog.

What did the elder chimney say to the younger chimney?

You're too young to smoke!

What did one hat say to another?

You stay here, I'll go on a head.

Why couldn't dracula's wife get to sleep?

Because of his coffin.

What did the worker at the rubber band factory say when he lost his job?

Oh Snap!

Why are pirates called pirates?

Cause they arrrrr.

What do prisoners use to call each other?

Cell phones.

What three candies can you find in every school?

Nerds, DumDums, and smarties.

How many books can you put in an empty backpack?

One! After that it's not empty!

What did the lawyer name his daughter?

Sue.

What did the cat say after eating two robins lying in the sun?

I just love baskin' robins.

How do crazy people go through the forest?

They take the psycho path.

Did you hear they're changing the flooring in daycare centers?

They're calling it infant-tile!

Why did the cookie go to the hospital?

Because he felt crummy.

Why did Johnny throw the clock out of the window?

Because he wanted to see time fly!

After Monday and Tuesday even the calendar says W T F.

What did one ocean say to the other ocean?

Nothing, they just waved.

The dyslexic devil worshipper sold his soul to Santa.

I hate Russian dolls, they're so full of themselves.

A computer once beat me at chess, but it was no match for me at kick boxing.

When I see birds fly, I think to myself: **"If I was a bird, who would I make a poo on?"**

As long as there are tests, there will be prayer in schools.

You kill vegetarian vampires with a steak to the heart.

What is faster Hot or cold?
Hot, because you can catch a cold.

I don't know if liquor is the answer, but it's worth a shot!

For Sale: Parachute. Only used once, never opened.

I asked my North Korean friend how it was there, he said he couldn't complain.

If you want to catch a squirrel just climb a tree and act like a nut.

I haven't talked to my wife in three weeks. I didn't want to interrupt her.

A day without sunshine is like, night.

Not saying I hate you, but if your face was on fire and I had a glass of water I'd drink it.

My wife and I were happy for twenty years; then we met.

Born free, taxed to death.

Why can't a bike stand on its own?
It's two tired.

Throwing acid is wrong, in some people's eyes.

What's the difference between a new husband and a new dog?
After a year, the dog is still excited to see you.

My favorite part of a marathon is watching the reaction of runners who grab my plastic cup of vodka.

I haven't slept for three days, because that would be too long.

A bank is a place that will lend you money, if you can prove that you don't need it.

PMS should just be called ovary-acting.

The nice thing about being senile is you can hide your own Easter eggs.

My friend gave me his Epi-Pen as he was dying.

It seemed very important to him that I have it.

I used to have winter fat but now I have spring rolls.

Love may be blind, but marriage is a real eye-opener.

Pampered cows produce spoiled milk.

I saw a sign that said "watch for children" and I thought,

"That sounds like a fair trade."

Why is it so hard for women to find men that are sensitive, caring, and good-looking?

Because those men already have boyfriends.

I heard a great joke about amnesia but I forgot it.

What's the difference between a paycheck and a pen*s?

You don't have to beg your wife to blow your paycheck.

People say I'm condescending.

That means i talk down to people.

Learn sign language, it's very handy.

When everything's coming your way, you're in the wrong lane.

A diplomat is someone who can tell you to go to hell in such a way that you will look forward to the trip.

Why did the scientist install a knocker on his door?

He wanted to win the No-bell prize!

I was at an ATM and this old lady asked me to help check her balance, so I pushed her over.

Dwarfs and midgets have very little in common.

Why do men find it difficult to make eye contact?

Breasts don't have eyes.

Good friends are like bottles of Sweet Wine......that's why I keep mine locked in the cellar.

What do you call a boomerang that doesn't come back?
A stick.

I am a nobody, nobody is perfect, therefore I am perfect.

I wondered why the frisbee was getting bigger, and then it hit me.

Whenever I find the key to success, someone changes the lock.

With great power, comes great electricity bills.

One snowman asks another, **"Do you smell carrots?"**

I say no to alcohol, it just doesn't listen.

If you can't convince them, confuse them.

The Gym is like Church. **Everybody thinks that by going one hour, one day, they'll erase what they did during the week.**

Why is the man who invests all your money called a broker?

If 4 out of 5 people SUFFER from diarrhea; does that mean that one enjoys it?

Why did the bee get married?
Because he found his honey.

A bartender is just a pharmacist with a limited inventory.

Violence is never the answer.
It's just a really good solution.

Eat right. Stay fit. Die anyway.

I used to like my neighbors, until they put a password on their Wi-Fi.

Lottery: a tax on people who are bad at math.

Current relationship status:
Made dinner for two. Ate both.

My birth certificate was a letter of apology that my dad got from the condom company.

For anyone who think a woman's place is in the kitchen, remember that's where the knives are kept.

Time is what keeps things from happening all at once.

If practice makes perfect, and nobody's perfect, why practice?

I won $3 million on the lottery this weekend so I decided to donate a quarter of it to charity.
Now I have $2,999,999.75.

I just let my mind wander, and it didn't come back.

Doctor: You're overweight. Patient: I think I want a second opinion.
Doctor: You're also ugly.

If at first you don't succeed, destroy all evidence that you tried.

Ain't it funny how the colors red, white, and blue represent freedom until they are flashing behind your car.

Why do farts smell?

So deaf people can enjoy them too.

You cannot taste me, until you undress me. (Banana)

A recent study has found that women who carry a little extra weight live longer than the men who mention it.

IRS: We've got what it takes to take what you have got.

You know you're ugly when it comes to a group picture and they hand you the camera.

What do you call a sheep with no legs? A cloud.

I can handle pain until it hurts.

How do you seduce a fat woman? **Piece of cake.**

You cannot eat me unless you lick me. (Ice-cream)

Whenever you get mad, just think of a t-rex trying to dance ballet.

A bargain is something you don't need at a price you can't resist.

What happens when you get scared half to death twice?

Sometimes we expect more from others because we would be willing to do that much more for them.

Isn't it weird how when a cop drives by you feel paranoid instead of protected.

Do not argue with an idiot.
He will drag you down to his level and beat you with experience.

How can you tell when a lawyer is lying? – **His lips are moving.**

THANK YOU!

www.ingramcontent.com/pod-product-compliance
Ingram Content Group UK Ltd.
Pitfield, Milton Keynes, MK11 3LW, UK
UKHW032214171224
452513UK00010B/552